DAMN YOU ANXIETY
USING LOGOSYNTHESIS® TO MANAGE LIFE'S CHALLENGES

DAMN YOU ANXIETY

USING LOGOSYNTHESIS® TO MANAGE LIFE'S CHALLENGES

Myriam Nordemann
& Allen O'Donoghue

DAMN YOU ANXIETY
USING LOGOSYNTHESIS® TO MANAGE LIFE'S CHALLENGES

©2023 by Myriam Nordemann & Allen O'Donoghue
All rights reserved - most notably those of reproduction, distribution, and translation.

Logosynthesis® and translations of this term are registered trademarks of Dr. Willem Lammers, and may not be used without his expressed prior consent.

Designed by Fowler Publishing Services

ISBN - 978-1-8382593-4-1

TABLE OF CONTENTS

Introduction 1
   Why was I given this book? 1
   How this book can help you 1
   Some basic information 2

Yourself 5
   Self Confidence 6
   Self Esteem 12
   Body Image 17
   Identity 23

Yourself & Others 26
   Family 27
   Friends 33
   Intimate Relationships 39
   Other Adults 45

Yourself & Your Future 51
   Studies 52
   Work 58
   Future Anxiety 64
   Love 69
   Potential 75

Conclusion 79
   What parents need to know 80
   What is Logosynthesis® 80
   Get in touch 81

Acknowledgements 83

INTRODUCTION

Why was I given this book?

There is a good chance you are reading this and thinking, "Why the F*&K did my parents give me this?", "I'm willing to give this a shot because I just want to feel better", or maybe you're somewhere in between.

We know you may not be sure if or how this workbook might help you, but if you're open to giving it a try, we are confident you'll find it useful and feel more in control of your thoughts and emotions.

The benefit of this workbook is that you can dip in and out of it and focus on the chapters that are important for you right now, and leave the others until you need them, if you ever do.

How this book can help you.

The beauty of the Logosynthesis® Basic Procedure is that it is a simple model to use and is a powerful tool in helping us manage our anxiety and stress levels. The proper way to describe it is that we use the power of words to get rid of emotional blockages. "WHAT??" we hear you cry. Well let's explain it this way, have you ever had someone hurt your feelings and then had the memories make you feel bad long after the event? Have you got a phobia of dogs after being bitten as a child, yet you've never been bitten again? Have you had a teacher tell you you're not good at maths and seen your results go downhill? All of these events happen and then they are over, yet they play on our minds, cause us anxiety and make us feel less confident. What has happened is that in the moment that the words were spoken, the bite took place or whatever has happened to you, your energy became blocked. The Logosynthesis® Basic Procedure uses specific sentences to remove these blocks and allow your energy to flow freely, which reduces the fear, stress, or anxiety we experience.

It's important to understand that anxiety is not a disease. It is a normal, natural emotional state that every human being experiences.

Anxiety is also an emotion of the future. We can either worry about an unknown "something" happening or focus on a past event that we think will occur again. Basically we fixate on a worst case scenario. This can then stop us from being happy and content in the here and now.

We have separated the workbook up into three sections that will focus on different areas that many people can find challenging as they grow up.

One of the most important elements of this whole process is to give yourself some time. We are living through an amazing period in history with technology placing almost everything at our fingertips. However, it can sometimes be hard to switch off from our devices because they can help us keep connected with the people we care about. This is where our anxiety and stress levels can go up, as we fear we will miss out on what is happening with our friends or the world around us.

With the techniques in this workbook, if you allow yourself the time to go through the steps and overall process, it can give you a better chance of fully resolving whatever issue you are experiencing right now. It may take five minutes or an hour, but by giving yourself permission to pause everything else and focus on feeling better, you are beginning to take care of yourself.

For example, imagine you break your arm. You need to take pain medication for as long as the doctor tells you. You need to stop doing some activities until it is healed. You are required to make the time to see the doctor for follow up visits. While all of this can be frustrating, it is worth it and will help you with a full recovery. With negative beliefs or trauma, we carry on living as best as we can but rarely try to deal with them or get rid of the blockages, as it can be scary. In our experience, when we give ourselves that time to heal, it can have a profound impact on our lives right now and into the future.

You deserve to not be held back by limiting beliefs and blockages. In order to do this, it is so important to look at how we can control things for ourselves rather than "blaming" the world and feeling powerless to change our personal situation. Yes, your parents might be a pain in the ass. Yes, they may be a major cause of your stress and anxiety, but pointing a finger at them doesn't help you feel better. It's time to take control of your own thoughts and actions, so you're in control of whether you feel good or not!

Some basic information

Mission
One of the basic assumptions in Logosynthesis® is that every person on this planet has a mission or purpose, a reason to be here. Many of our clients have come to us as they struggle to see any purpose to their lives or any future possibilities. We're here to say we understand and, trust us, you will find your purpose at some point. It's okay to not know what this might be, right now. It will all become clear and you DO have a reason to be here.

Beliefs
One of the reasons we may struggle to figure out our purpose is down to the beliefs we have taken on throughout our lives, which can cloud our view of ourselves and the world around us (e.g. a teacher tells us we are not very good at maths and we believe it and then tell the world that we are not good at maths). We can question our potential and limit ourselves greatly. As stated earlier, there will be some positive beliefs that help us live in society, but others can block us. We take on beliefs as young children to help us make sense of the world and to stay alive. As we grow, we don't need many of these beliefs as we learn to take care of ourselves, but when we are under stress, we can go back to the beliefs we used to have as children. In this workbook we will help you to reduce the impact of the beliefs that you don't need any more, so you can begin to work towards your purpose and feel more in flow.

Mental Health
Mental health is one of the biggest things talked about in society right now, which is really positive. One

of the challenges we have found is that people can sometimes not know what are just "regular" challenges that we all have to deal with (e.g. not wanting to get up for school in the morning because we are tired) and what is a struggle that needs more in depth support, such as counselling or therapy (thoughts of self harm, deep depression, etc). We have found working with young people, in some cases, it can only take a few sessions for a person to feel more confident in coping with life's ups and downs.

Gratitude

Gratitude is so important in helping us maintain a positive outlook. We can be conditioned to look at what others have or do and be envious and forget that we have so much in our own lives to be grateful for. That's not to say that we don't have significant challenges and hurts, but if we continually focus on these, we will only see the negative side of life. I remember listening to the wonderful philosopher and neuroscientist, Sam Harris, talking about how, if we were to experience something devastatingly traumatic right now, the chances are, we would give all the money in the world to go back and have the challenges of yesterday. Taking 5 minutes every morning to recognise the parts of our lives that we can be grateful for, no matter how seemingly insignificant, can have such a powerful impact on our perspective in life.

Gremlin

One of the ways we can figure out the negative beliefs is to listen out for our gremlin. Every one of us has a gremlin that just wants us to stay exactly as we are and not to make any changes at all. We will hear our gremlin tell us not to try new things, let us know we're not good enough to achieve something we want, and our gremlin knows our deepest, darkest fears and how to trigger us!

By listening out for your gremlin's voice, you may get some clues as to what topics you might work on with this workbook.

For a bit of fun, why not draw your own gremlin. It can be as ugly or artistic as you like and then you can begin to tell your gremlin that you won't be listening to it today.

Okay, are you ready? Let's jump right in.
Draw a mind map of all the things causing you stress right now. Pick one to start with and give yourself some time to work through it and see how you get on. Find the section in your workbook that matches your issue closest and go for it. If you find it a bit weird to start, that's okay, stick with it and the more you do the exercises, the more skilled you will become at managing your thoughts, emotions and behaviours.

Why have we picked the three sections below?

Yourself:
Put on your own mask first! In order to be able to help those we care about, we need to take care of ourselves equally as much. This doesn't mean becoming selfish, but recognising that if we constantly put others first, we drain our own resources, which ultimately isn't good for anyone! This section looks at how we can overcome our own internal challenges and feel more confident in the world.

Yourself & Others:
The people around us are important and can help us in so many ways, yet we can worry or be anxious about our relationships with them. This section helps you to remove unnecessary blockages you may have with the different people in your life, past and present.

Yourself & Your Future:
Anxiety is an emotion of the future. We can worry about what might happen (and usually think of the worst case scenario!) and this can stop us from doing things in the here and now, even though the issue we are worried about hasn't even happened yet, AND it is highly unlikely to be as bad as we expect. With this section, we remove the anxieties of the future, which will help you build the future you want.

YOURSELF

YOU

SELF-CONFIDENCE

Self-confidence is a basic feeling of trust in ourselves and our ability to handle things. We are neither "confident" or "not confident", our confidence will flow up and down depending on what we are doing and how we are doing it. We can be confident in our ability to do certain things we are good at, while we may need to work on and practise to improve in other areas. When we are not confident in ourselves, we can doubt our ability to face obstacles and challenges, we can struggle to trust ourselves, or we can completely shut down and feel like we can't move forward. The thing to remember is that these doubts are just blockages that we can get rid of. Let's show you how with the next two exercises.

Activity 1: Accepting Myself

When we are confident, we accept our thoughts, behaviours and attitudes. But in reality we often get angry at ourselves for how we think, what we do and how we are.

Throughout this workbook, you will see a Notes section after each activity, so use it as you need to.

For this exercise, we want you to write down the judgements you have about yourself that are not helpful for your life (This is for you to write down whatever you feel is important, including triggers, level of distress these triggers cause or any other elements you think are relevant). Look for the worst things you think about yourself in terms of who you are and how you act.

For example:

"My thoughts are: stupid, complicated, a mistake…"

"What I do is: useless, always wrong, ridiculous…"

"I am: a failure, a disaster, incapable…"

Please indicate from 0 to 10 (0 being the lowest distress it causes you, 10 being the highest) how true you believe each of these statements to be.

Notice what is happening in your body, your emotions and your thoughts.

Then apply the sentences of the Logosynthesis® Basic Procedure below to each of those judgments starting with the one you feel the strongest reaction to. It is essential to never apply the sentences to an emotion, as the emotion is a legitimate response to what is triggering you. If you work on the emotion, then you are not working on the actual issue. For example, if you are sad that your coach said you had a terrible game, there is nothing wrong with this emotional response, but if you find that it is making you think, "I am never good enough in anything I do", this is the belief to work on. Pick a representation of that emotion, (belief, memory, thought, image, sound, smell etc) and apply the sentences to this instead.

For example, if I believe I am never good enough at anything I do, I would use the following sentences:

I retrieve, all my energy, bound up in the belief that I am never good enough at anything, and all it represents, and take it to the right place in myself. (Pause here to allow the words to work)

I remove, all non-me energy, related to the belief that I am never good enough at anything, and all it represents, from all my cells, all my body and my personal space, and send it where it truly belongs. (Pause here to allow the words to work)

I retrieve, all my energy, bound up in all my reactions, to the belief that I am never good enough at anything, and all it represents, and take it, to the right place in myself. (Pause here to allow the words to work)

Apply the sentences, one by one, to each statement until you are down to 0. If you don't get down to a 0 after the first round, check in with yourself and see what number you have got to, maybe a 6, and ask yourself, what is keeping this at a 6? Then do the sentences again, but this time put in the new representation that you have discovered by asking what is keeping it at a 6.

Sentences of the Logosynthesis® Basic Procedure:

I retrieve, all my energy, bound up in X (the representation), and all it represents, and take it to the right place in myself. (Pause here to allow the words to work)

I remove, all non-me energy, related to X (the representation), and all it represents, from all my cells, all my body and my personal space, and send it where it truly belongs. (Pause here to allow the words to work)

I retrieve, all my energy, bound up in all my reactions, to X (the representation), and all it represents, and take it, to the right place in myself. (Pause here to allow the words to work)

Notice what happens to you when you get to 0. Also, don't be in a rush to get them all down to a 0 right now, take your time.

When you get to 0, repeat the following sentence: *I attune, all my systems, to this new awareness.*

NOTES

Activity 2: Connecting to My Intuition

When you have confidence, you know you have the resources to move forward and deal with many situations.

We all have that little voice inside us that knows what is good for us. It is our intuition, that makes us trust in our choices. It is important to listen to this wisdom within ourselves. Yet all too often we are conditioned to question this voice by the judgements of those around us and our internal gremlin.

Let's draw an image that represents this intuition. Now draw images for the other voices around you (parents, siblings, teachers, coaches etc).

Represent each image with colours, strokes, symbols, shapes and or words, whatever works for you.

Then give your drawing a title and look at it. What emotions come up for you when you look at the images (about yourself, others, the world)?

Do you experience discomfort in your body? What thoughts or memories come to mind?

Now rate your level of discomfort from 0 to 10 for each image. Observe in your drawing what causes you the most stress.

If it is a line, a colour, a detail, apply the sentences of the Logosynthesis® Basic Procedure below to that detail that you have highlighted and that is of greatest stress, giving pause time in between each sentence.

Sentences of the Logosynthesis® Basic Procedure:

I retrieve, all my energy, bound up in X (the representation), and all it represents, and take it to the right place in myself. (Pause here to allow the words to work)

I remove, all non-me energy, related to X (the representation), and all it represents, from all my cells, all my body and my personal space, and send it where it truly belongs. (Pause here to allow the words to work)

I retrieve, all my energy, bound up in all my reactions, to X (the representation), and all it represents, and take it, to the right place in myself. (Pause here to allow the words to work)

What has changed? Now, what is your stress level from 0 to 10?

Notice the changes and the new stress level. If it is not at 0, repeat the procedure with new representations each time. If you find you are struggling to get to 0, you can also leave it for now. Sometimes getting to a 1 or a 2 is sufficient for us to be more confident in managing life in the here and now. You can always come back to the issue if you need to.

When you get to 0 repeat the following sentence: *I attune, all my systems, to this new awareness.*

NOTES

SELF-ESTEEM

Activity 1: Self-esteem according to...

Self-esteem is essentially how we value and see ourselves in relation to the world around us. Throughout the day our level of self-esteem can vary depending on who we meet, what we do, what happens. Now we will work on the situations where the level of self-esteem is low.

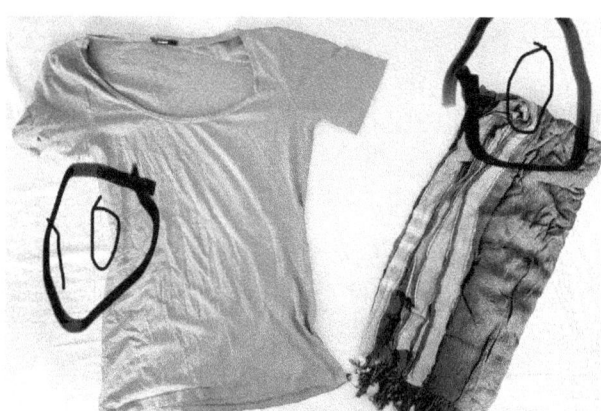

For this activity open your wardrobe and choose an outfit that represents your highest self-esteem value i.e. 100. Then choose another outfit that represents your lowest level, possibly 1, which is when your inner dialogue or an experience or interaction with someone causes you to lose belief in yourself. I (Myriam) picked a scarf that I have never worn, as I don't like to have something wrapped around my neck.

Say the sentences of the Logosynthesis® Basic Procedure about the clothing that gives you low self-esteem and everything it represents.

Sentences of the Logosynthesis® Basic Procedure:

I retrieve, all my energy, bound up in X (the representation), and all it represents, and take it to the right place in myself. (Pause here to allow the words to work)

I remove, all non-me energy, related to X (the representation), and all it represents, from all my cells, all my body and my personal space, and send it where it truly belongs. (Pause here to allow the words to work)

I retrieve, all my energy, bound up in all my reactions, to X (the representation), and all it represents, and take it, to the right place in myself. (Pause here to allow the words to work)

When you get to 0 repeat the following sentence: *I attune, all my systems, to this new awareness.*

Observe what has changed. As for me, I now like this scarf (which I've never worn) and want to wear it along with my shirt to feel even better! How about you?

NOTES

Activity 2: I am...

Our inner dialogues often cause us suffering and can bring us down. When we let go of the thoughts that keep us from being bright, feeling good and confident, we change and can experience joy and happiness.

On a piece of paper make a circle representing your face. At the level of what would be the forehead, write "I am..." and then continue with all the emotionally painful adjectives that come to mind.

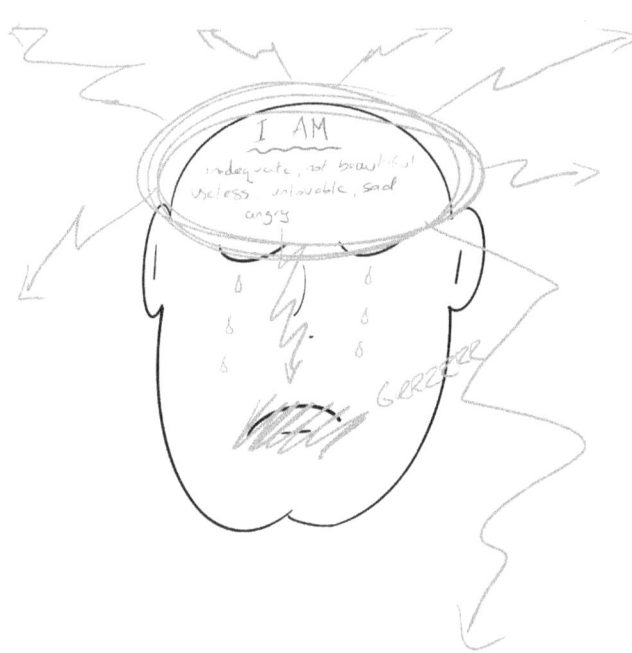

Then draw facial features, and from the forehead make arrows that represent the energy that directs these thoughts outward, toward others, or within yourself. In the example I have put arrows that, like lightning bolts, go outwards, and arrows inside that go to the mouth and make it spit blood from anger!!!!!

Assess your stress level related to drawing between 0-10 and now say the sentences of the Logosynthesis® Basic Procedure below.

Sentences of the Logosynthesis® Basic Procedure:

I retrieve, all my energy, bound up in X (the representation), and all it represents, and take it to the right place in myself. (Pause here to allow the words to work)

I remove, all non-me energy, related to X (the representation), and all it represents, from all my cells, all my body and my personal space, and send it where it truly belongs. (Pause here to allow the words to work)

I retrieve, all my energy, bound up in all my reactions, to X (the representation), and all it represents, and take it, to the right place in myself. (Pause here to allow the words to work)

Reassess your new stress level. If it is at 0, the job is done, and you can move to the fourth sentence, *I attune, all my systems, to this new awareness*. If the score is higher, find out what detail is causing it and say the sentences about what this is. Ask yourself, what is keeping it up at X?

Example: *"I retrieve all my energy related to these crying eyes and everything it represents…"*

Proceed with all the details of the drawing until your stress level is at zero.

NOTES

BODY IMAGE

Activity 1: My Body

As a teenager your body changes quickly, you can feel happy with some of these changes and that is a pleasant thing, but they can also be a source of discomfort, shame, pain. At this stage of life, we can feel like everyone is looking at us and we may feel that we are different and no longer recognize ourselves.

I remember, in my adolescence, the thousands of thoughts, the concern to hide moles, pimples and intrusive hair, my curved shoulders to hide a prosperous breast and the observation of a friend of my father, when I was 16 years old, at the beach, about my cellulite… were daily torments with which I struggled to live peacefully.

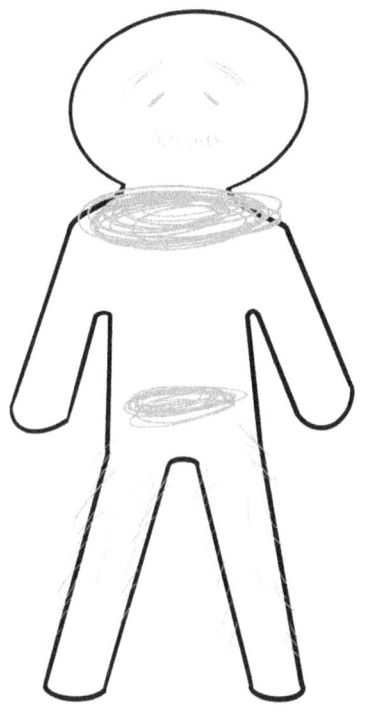

For this activity I suggest you highlight the parts of your body that you have difficulty relating to.

On a blank sheet of paper draw a silhouette of your body with a marker of the colour of your choice.

Take another marker of a different colour and mark with strokes, lines and scribbles all the parts where you feel tension, difficulty, discomfort of any kind. In the picture I marked them in red.

Mark next to each part of your body where you feel discomfort, an indicator of stress from 0 to 10. For me, for example, it's 10 for my shoulders, 8 for my thighs, 6 for my face. You can go into more detail, rating for example your eyes, middle part of your face, right leg, etc.

Observe where there is discomfort and what emotions, thoughts, tensions in the body that cause it.

Say the sentences of the Logosynthesis® Basic Procedure about each of these body parts, starting with the one with the highest number.

Sentences of the Logosynthesis® Basic Procedure:

I retrieve, all my energy, bound up in X (the representation), and all it represents, and take it to the right place in myself. (Pause here to allow the words to work)

I remove, all non-me energy, related to X (the representation), and all it represents, from all my cells, all my body and my personal space, and send it where it truly belongs. (Pause here to allow the words to work)

I retrieve, all my energy, bound up in all my reactions, to X (the representation), and all it represents, and take it, to the right place in myself. (Pause here to allow the words to work)

Now re-evaluate your stress level from 0 to 10 for each body part and say the sentences again about those body parts where you still feel discomfort. Do this until the discomfort has dropped to around 0 throughout the body.

At 0, repeat the following sentence: *I attune, all my systems, to this new awareness.*

Now design your silhouette again. What has changed?
For me, it changed like this! Now find out what happens when you reconnect with your body and when you observe it. What changes?

NOTES

Activity 2: Me and Others

From the time we are young, we become aware of physical differences in people and also with the idealised images of culture (celebrities, sports stars, etc). In this way we build up an idea of what is beautiful and healthy and what is not. Some bodies attract us, others repel us. Many of us would like to resemble a model — we can compare ourselves, we can work hard to get closer to it and then we can feel demoralised and bad about ourselves when we compare it to our current body shape. We can disconnect from reality, but are stuck in pictures and ideas of bodies that may not exist or can be unattainable for many. Even the most "beautiful" people can find fault in their own appearance.

For this activity we're going to ask you to go online and print out images or get some magazines and a pair of scissors and glue, and build a collage of photographs of bodies of the gender you identify with as I did in the figure.

Let your instincts and emotional reactions, not necessarily just positive or negative ones, guide you. Whether the image of a body causes you revulsion or envy, can be a sign that there is work to be done!

Now look at your collage and identify which body causes you the most discomfort. What emotion is present when you look at this photo? What do you think? What are the sensations in your body? Rate the degree of stress from 0 to 10 and say the sentences of the Logosynthesis® Basic Procedure about this photo and everything it represents.

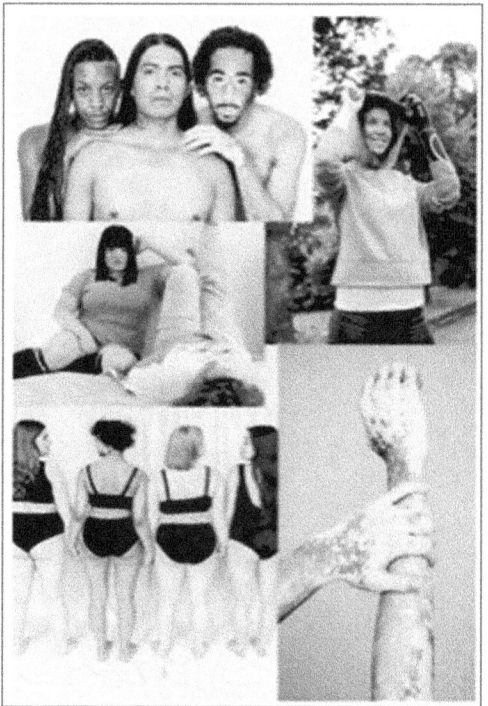

Photo credits via pexels.com:
Antoni Shkraba, Polina Tankilevitch, Armin Rimoldi, and RF._.studio

Sentences of the Logosynthesis® Basic Procedure:

I retrieve, all my energy, bound up in X (the representation), and all it represents, and take it to the right place in myself. (Pause here to allow the words to work)

I remove, all non-me energy, related to X (the representation), and all it represents, from all my cells, all my body and my personal space, and send it where it truly belongs. (Pause here to allow the words to work)

I retrieve, all my energy, bound up in all my reactions, to X (the representation), and all it represents, and take it, to the right place in myself. (Pause here to allow the words to work)

What happens now? Has something changed? Do you still feel discomfort? If you no longer feel discomfort, repeat the exercise on another body. If you still feel uncomfortable, find out what part of that body is bothering you? Is it the belly? Is it the hair? Is it because the person is overweight or too thin? Rate from 0 to 10 the discomfort that this detail creates for you and say the sentences of the Logosynthesis® Basic Procedure about it and everything it represents.

What has changed? If the body no longer bothers you, move on to another one and repeat the exercise. If that body still causes you discomfort, repeat the exercise on a new one. Go on until the whole collage has become emotionally neutral for you.

Don't forget, if you get to 0, repeat the fourth sentence: *I attune, all my systems, to this new awareness.*

NOTES

IDENTITY

Many of us, as teenagers, can go through a process of trying to understand our own sexuality. We can question ourselves a lot, and the feelings that come and go, like huge waves, and it's so important to know that this is absolutely okay and normal. It can feel like a very lonely place at times and if we are unsure of how our friends or family might react, it can be scary to even think about going against what people see as "normal".

The first thing to remember is that so many people across the world have experienced something similar and you are not alone. Thankfully, exploring your gender and sexuality has become more and more acceptable, and even encouraged, and there is generally a greater understanding for people going through this journey.

We completely understand that us stating "it's okay" doesn't mean you will just FEEL that it is okay. If you are going through a challenging time, wondering, questioning, here is an exercise that can help make some room inside you, to be more okay with exploring your own gender and sexuality.

Grab a sheet of paper, and write ME at the bottom of the page. Then MALE, FEMALE & NON-BINARY at the top of the page. After that, write down all of the things that you believe are standing in the way of your journey to discover or just play around with different identities.

Now sit and look at the words you've written that are blocking your path and see which one jumps out as having the strongest impact on you. Now rate, on a scale of 0 - 10, what is the level of distress it causes you. If an image or picture comes to mind in relation to the blockage, say the sentences of the Logosynthesis® Basic Procedure using this image or picture.

Sentences of the Logosynthesis® Basic Procedure:

I retrieve, all my energy, bound up in X (the representation), and all it represents, and take it to the right place in myself. (Pause here to allow the words to work)

I remove, all non-me energy, related to X (the representation), and all it represents, from all my cells, all my body and my personal space, and send it where it truly belongs. (Pause here to allow the words to work)

I retrieve, all my energy, bound up in all my reactions, to X (the representation), and all it represents, and take it, to the right place in myself. (Pause here to allow the words to work)

After doing the sentences, check in with what is going on inside. Has the level of distress reduced. If any new images or representation popped into your head while you were saying the sentences, and your level of distress has not got down to a 0, do another round of sentences based on the new representation!

When you get to 0, repeat the following sentence: *I attune, all my systems, to this new awareness.*

NOTES

YOURSELF & OTHERS

FAMILY

Activity 1: Clean Up Your Roots

Have you done your family tree yet? If you haven't, now is your chance! You might ask, "Why would I do this?". Sometimes, traumas and phobias can be passed down through generations. We may not KNOW why something is uncomfortable or scary, but we FEEL the emotion. By doing this exercise we can resolve issues that may not actually be from something that has happened to us, but they are impacting us on an emotional level.

I did my family tree for the first time when I was about twenty-five years old and it was an exciting and enriching experience, a great opportunity to look for photos and discover many anecdotes and untold stories about the lives of relatives and ancestors. It has also helped me connect faces and names, relocate some stories heard with distracted ears in the past, and feel stronger connections to some family members.

Recently, a 15-year-old client of mine, distressed by fear of death from cancer, discovered a special connection to her great-grandmother, who died of this very disease.

Speaking the sentences of the Logosynthesis® Basic Procedure for her was a real relief! Besides overcoming her fear, they helped her to detach herself from the life and destiny of this relative, even though she still felt her presence very strongly. At the end of the meeting she told me: "It's as if my great-grandmother was here with me, watching me and supporting me".

Are you ready?

Take a large sheet of white paper (70x80 cm for example).

Then, some coloured markers.

Start by creating your family tree. For this exercise we will do it for the people in your immediate family. There is nothing stopping you from making a larger family tree, including uncles, aunts, cousins....

So indicate your name, then those of your parents, grandparents, great-grandparents, brothers and sisters, just like in the example below.

If you have in-laws and are part of an extended family indicate those with whom you are most familiar as well.

You can write some quick notes about them

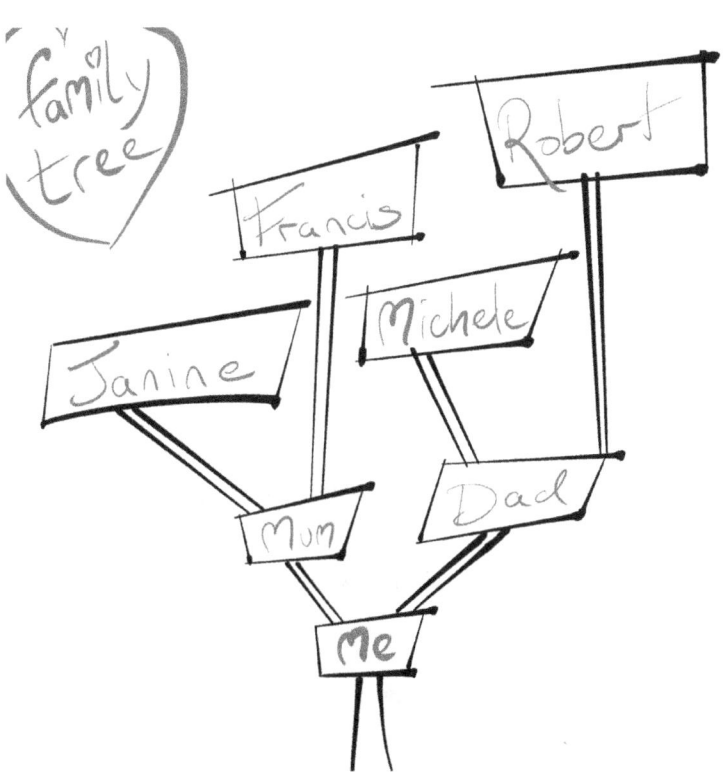

(birth/important fact of their life/death).

If you have pictures, paste them next to the corresponding names!

Now place your finger on the paper at your name.

Explore what you feel inside when you look at the other people arranged on the tree.

To whom do you feel the most connection to? Or tension? Or discomfort?

Where do you feel these emotions in your body?

Stop for a moment just on the feeling of discomfort. Where do you feel it within your body?

Indicate your level of discomfort by writing next to each person a score from 0 to 10 with a red marker.

Check which person you feel most uncomfortable with.

Speak the following sentences of the Logosynthesis® Basic Procedure:

> ### Sentences of the Logosynthesis® Basic Procedure:
>
> *I retrieve, all my energy, bound up in X (the representation), and all it represents, and take it to the right place in myself.* (Pause here to allow the words to work)
>
> *I remove, all non-me energy, related to X (the representation), and all it represents, from all my cells, all my body and my personal space, and send it where it truly belongs.* (Pause here to allow the words to work)
>
> *I retrieve, all my energy, bound up in all my reactions, to X (the representation), and all it represents, and take it, to the right place in myself.* (Pause here to allow the words to work)

Observe what is going on inside of you.

Now what is your stress level (always from 0 to 10)? What do you experience now in your body and through your emotions when you connect with this relative?

Repeat the exercise until your discomfort with this person reaches 0.

Then move on to the relative with the next stress indicator and repeat the sentence: *I attune, all my systems, to this new awareness.*

NOTES

Activity 2:
Your story with...

A relationship with another person is built over years. There can be good times and more difficult times. With each of my family I have good and bad memories.

I have an infinite tenderness and love for my father, yet when I think of him besides the laughter and trust, I also remember his disapproving look and moments in which I felt deeply rejected and hurt.

If these moments and representations are still "active" in my personal space all my energy is not in the present of the relationship. I am conditioned by the past, a part of me is as if I am still trapped by these memories. Using the sentences of the Logosynthesis® Basic Procedure will help you neutralise them and live in the present moment of the relationship. If the person is deceased, it will allow you to integrate these events into your present experience.

I propose that you go through your history with the other person and "clear" it, working on the difficult emotions that arise from your memories and freeing them from incomplete and unintegrated emotions. Choose one person you want to work on. It can be your brother or sister, your mom or dad.

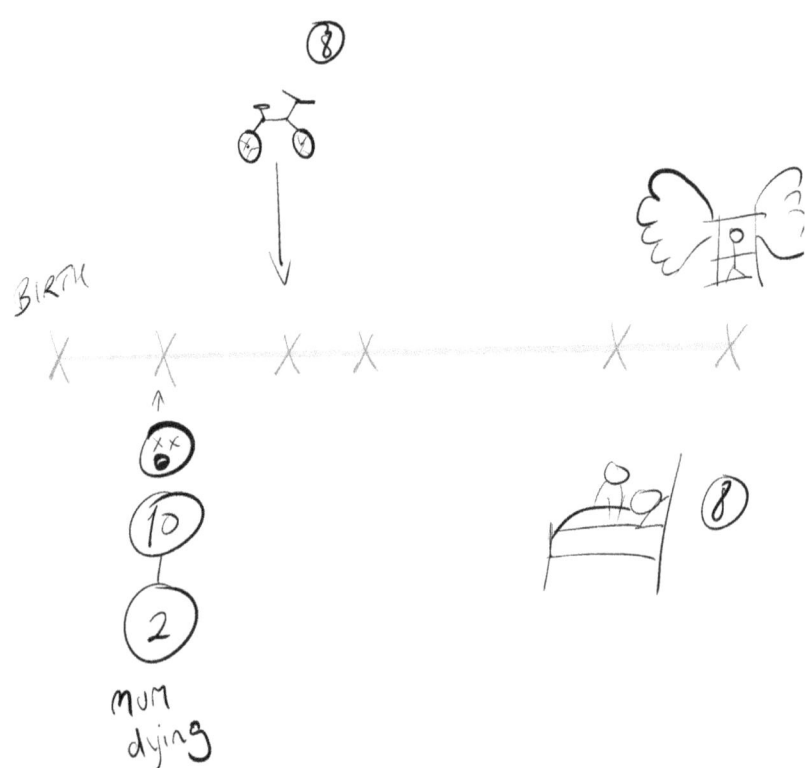

Draw a timeline like the example above. This line indicates the development of your relationship over time.

The beginning of the line indicates the first time you met. For parents and older siblings, the story begins with your conception. Indeed, according to the beliefs of Logosynthesis®, with the moment your Essence decided to come to earth. It doesn't matter: just write down that it's the beginning of the relationship.

On the line, place the highlights of your relationship and associate a small drawing, doodle or symbol that represents this moment. For example, on my relationship line with my maternal grandmother, Janine, I indicated when my mom died (my mum died when I was 1 year old) and I symbolised it with a screaming face; then, in the moment of my adolescence, when I went to visit my grandmother on my bicycle (I really drew a bicycle!); when I went to live in Italy and that I felt that it could be the last embrace, that there was the possibility that we would not see each other anymore, and I symbolised it with a door and huge arms that want to welcome me. Finally, I drew her in her bed in the last days of her life.

Explore for each point represented, what happens to you? What emotions do you experience? What is going on inside you? Next to each event/symbol put your level of discomfort, from 0 to 10, where 10 is the highest distress you experience.

Now begin to say the sentences about the event where the stress is highest by indicating it in the sentence with its object symbol (e.g. I retrieve, all my energy, bound up in this bicycle and all it represents…).

Sentences of the Logosynthesis® Basic Procedure:

I retrieve, all my energy, bound up in X (the representation), and all it represents, and take it to the right place in myself. (Pause here to allow the words to work)

I remove, all non-me energy, related to X (the representation), and all it represents, from all my cells, all my body and my personal space, and send it where it truly belongs. (Pause here to allow the words to work)

I retrieve, all my energy, bound up in all my reactions, to X (the representation), and all it represents, and take it, to the right place in myself. (Pause here to allow the words to work)

Observe what is going on inside you.

Now: what is your level of discomfort (always from 0 to 10) when you connect to the symbol representing the event? What do you experience now? Make a note of these experiences.

Repeat the exercise until your discomfort with this person reaches 0, then repeat the following sentence: *I attune, all my systems, to this new awareness.* Then move on to the event with the next stress indicator.

Repeat the exercise until your timeline is clean!

If you wish, you can repeat this exercise on other people in the family, following the same process.

NOTES

FRIENDS

Activity 1: Within the group

How do you feel in a group of your peers?

When I was your age, I had a hard time... From my adolescence I remember strong friendships, which sometimes betrayed me, a feeling of belonging to my close group of friends that made me feel good, and other feelings of exclusion, even from a group of girls in class who made fun of me and treated me badly when I was 16.

There were so many little and big triggers that filled my time each day with strong emotions, good and not so good, that were sometimes hard to live with. At the time, I would have loved to have known about Logosynthesis® to help me find a way to feel good and centred in my relationships! I suggest trying this exercise to "clear" what around you is disturbing you.

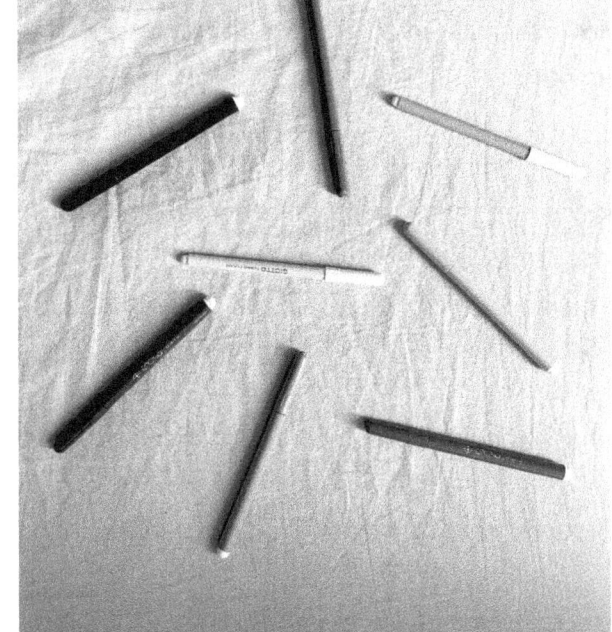

For this activity you will need coloured markers but no paper...we will use them as they are.

Choose a marker for yourself. The cap represents your head, the rest represents your body. Place it on a table in front of you.

The other markers represent your classmates, your friends, the people you hang out with, who are around you. Arrange these markers on the table. Follow your instincts. See how your hands and intuition help you arrange the various markers. It is not essential to specifically name each marker.

Place your hand on your marker. What is the present emotion and where do you experience it in your body?
What do you think about yourself? About others ? About life in general from this position?

What is your stress level from 0 to 10 ?

Identify which marker(s) cause you discomfort. For example: "the markers turned toward me that seem to be attacking me" or "the grey one away from me", or "the green one doesn't really impact me".

Now say the sentences of the Logosynthesis® Basic Procedure about what causes you the most discomfort.

Sentences of the Logosynthesis® Basic Procedure:

I retrieve, all my energy, bound up in X (the representation), and all it represents, and take it to the right place in myself. (Pause here to allow the words to work)

I remove, all non-me energy, related to X (the representation), and all it represents, from all my cells, all my body and my personal space, and send it where it truly belongs. (Pause here to allow the words to work)

I retrieve, all my energy, bound up in all my reactions, to X (the representation), and all it represents, and take it, to the right place in myself. (Pause here to allow the words to work)

Once you have said the three sentences and observed the three prescribed pause times, observe what has changed in you.

What do you want to do with the marker(s) you said the sentences on? Do you want to remove them ? Move them ? Do it! Remove the one(s) that are no longer appropriate and move the ones you feel like moving.

Now go back to the marker that represents you. What has changed? What emotions do you experience now when you look at the other markers? Where do you experience the emotions in your body ? What is your stress level now, from 0 to 10? Observe where this stress is coming from and start the process again until it is zero. When you get to 0, repeat the following sentence: *I attune, all my systems, to this new awareness.*

What happens now when you think about you and the group? What has changed?

Observe over the next few days what has changed about the group and others in general.

NOTES

Activity 2: A Bad Memory in a Friendship

Sometimes even with best friends you fight. And afterwards you can feel very bad. You don't know how to react, what to do, what to say, your emotions can take over and you can sometimes want to give up everything and something breaks in your heart and trust.

It happens at all ages - to me even today. Yesterday a friend of mine spoke to me in an aggressive way. I'm still not sure why, probably for her own reasons. She was nervous, tired or sad, and took it out on me.

Has this ever happened to you?

I invite you to think of a disagreement with one of your best friends and draw a picture in your Logosynthesis® notebook.

Draw with the marker two lines facing each other that represent you and the other person. Draw two faces with expressions appropriate to the situation. Around them draw what you felt, representing your emotions and how you see the other person.

Then rate from 0 to 10 the stress you feel when looking at your drawing.

What attracts your attention? What is the stress from? What colour? What shape? What stroke?

Here is the drawing I did for the fight with my friend.

Focus on what is most stressful (for me, in this drawing, the red around my face) and say the sentences of the Logosynthesis® Basic Procedure about the representation. Example: "I retrieve all my energy related to this colour red, and all it represents, and take it..."

Sentences of the Logosynthesis® Basic Procedure:

I retrieve, all my energy, bound up in X (the representation), and all it represents, and take it to the right place in myself. (Pause here to allow the words to work)

I remove, all non-me energy, related to X (the representation), and all it represents, from all my cells, all my body and my personal space, and send it where it truly belongs. (Pause here to allow the words to work)

I retrieve, all my energy, bound up in all my reactions, to X (the representation), and all it represents, and take it, to the right place in myself. (Pause here to allow the words to work)

After saying the sentences, what has changed in you? How high is your stress level? What is keeping it up at this new level?

Start the exercise again from another detail, or what is keeping it from being at a zero (for example, for me, it would be the other person's gaze).

Continue until the stress has dropped to 0. Once you get to 0, repeat the fourth sentence: *I attune, all my systems, to this new awareness.*

Think back to the argument with your loved one. What has changed? I now feel affection and tenderness for my friend. I feel it was just her moment and I love her even in this situation!

Also observe how your relationship with your friend changes after this work.

NOTES

INTIMATE RELATIONSHIP

Activity 1: My intimacy

Intimacy is the closeness that we build with other people. This can be mental, emotional or physical and develops over time. We become more comfortable with the other person and enjoy this closeness.

Intimacy is important to us as it lets us know that we are cared for, loved and accepted. This helps us build our sense of self worth.

Draw a circle.

Inside is your intimacy. Physical, emotional, mental. It is your world. Represent it. Draw your organs, your emotions, your thoughts. Observe what you have done and what it represents for you. What happens when you see it? What emotions do you feel? What thoughts? Where is the discomfort located in your body and what is it related to?

Then rate your stress level from 0 to 10 and apply the sentences of the Logosynthesis® Basic Procedure to what you have illustrated.

Sentences of the Logosynthesis® Basic Procedure:

I retrieve, all my energy, bound up in X (the representation), and all it represents, and take it to the right place in myself. (Pause here to allow the words to work)

I remove, all non-me energy, related to X (the representation), and all it represents, from all my cells, all my body and my personal space, and send it where it truly belongs. (Pause here to allow the words to work)

I retrieve, all my energy, bound up in all my reactions, to X (the representation), and all it represents, and take it, to the right place in myself. (Pause here to allow the words to work)

What has changed? What is your stress level from 0 to 10?

If you are not at 0, continue:

Observe in your drawing what causes you the most stress. If it is a line, a colour, a detail in the drawing, apply the sentences of the Logosynthesis® Basic Procedure to the detail you have highlighted that is of greatest stress.

Observe in your drawing what causes you the most discomfort. If it is not 0, repeat the procedure.

When you get to 0, repeat the following sentence: *I attune, all my systems, to this new awareness.*

NOTES

Activity 2: Who do I let into my intimacy?

Some of us may find it difficult to open ourselves up to developing an intimate relationship with someone else. This can be for a number of reasons, maybe we've been hurt or let down in the past, or we don't think we know how to be intimate.

There will always have to be a bit of trust and vulnerability to get into an intimate relationship with someone else and it can be hard to decide who to let in. This exercise can help to remove some blockages that may be there.

Draw a circle in the centre of your paper and inside it represent yourself. Then draw other people around you. Those who you see more. Place them at a greater or lesser distance from the circle depending on how close you want to bring them to your intimacy. A person you like can be drawn closer to you. A friend also. Someone else may have to stand further away.

Place your hand on the circle and find out what emotions come to you? It may be that some of the people depicted give you a little discomfort.

Observe this feeling. What emotions do you experience? What thoughts? Where is the discomfort in your body and what is it related to?

Then rate from 0 to 10 your level of stress related to this person and apply the sentences of the Logosynthesis® Basic Procedure to the whole representation.

Sentences of the Logosynthesis® Basic Procedure:

I retrieve, all my energy, bound up in X (the representation), and all it represents, and take it to the right place in myself. (Pause here to allow the words to work)

I remove, all non-me energy, related to X (the representation), and all it represents, from all my cells, all my body and my personal space, and send it where it truly belongs. (Pause here to allow the words to work)

I retrieve, all my energy, bound up in all my reactions, to X (the representation), and all it represents, and take it, to the right place in myself. (Pause here to allow the words to work)

What has changed? What is your stress level from 0 to 10?

If you are not at 0, continue with the process, observe in your drawing who causes you the most stress. Apply the sentences of the Logosynthesis® Basic Procedure to the person who evokes this feeling.

Observe the changes and the new level of discomfort. If you are not at 0, repeat the procedure.

If and when you get to 0, repeat the sentence: *I attune, all my systems, to this new awareness.*

NOTES

OTHER ADULTS
(Teachers, coach, people you admire etc)

Activity 1: The school of monsters

Even recently, I felt anxious at the memory of a teacher I named Levy who, when I was 13, frightened me when she was angry. Moody, unpredictable, feared by everyone. She had the ability, with her voice and look, to make me forget everything about the previous lesson!

We've all had amazing teachers and others a little less engaging. Some may have even made us hate their subject, while others have turned the subject we were strong in, into something boring, and still others have blocked us in our learning.

In this activity draw your school and the teachers or professors to forget! Draw the building, make windows and at each window doodle the teacher who yelled, discouraged you, bored you, etc... Observe what happens in your body, your emotions, your thoughts. Then rate the level of discomfort from 0 to 10 for each window.

Mine is like this... Professor Levy I put in the bottom left but my discomfort is only at 2 because I have already worked through my emotions related to her so much with Logosynthesis®, that thinking about her doesn't create the stress it used to! Instead, my Ancient Greek teacher is at 10 (my average in the subject was around 2/20) and I remember other teachers who seemed cold, unkempt and creepy!

Once you have identified the doodle and therefore the teacher that causes you the most discomfort, apply the sentences of the Logosynthesis® Basic Procedure to the drawing, and to everything it represents.

Sentences of the Logosynthesis® Basic Procedure:

I retrieve, all my energy, bound up in X (the representation), and all it represents, and take it to the right place in myself. (Pause here to allow the words to work)

I remove, all non-me energy, related to X (the representation), and all it represents, from all my cells, all my body and my personal space, and send it where it truly belongs. (Pause here to allow the words to work)

I retrieve, all my energy, bound up in all my reactions, to X (the representation), and all it represents, and take it, to the right place in myself. (Pause here to allow the words to work)

Now observe what has changed. What is your stress level from 0 to 10 about the representation of this person?

If your stress level is still high, you can see if there is a detail in the drawing that particularly activates you, for example the eyes, hair, or mouth, and say the sentences of the Logosynthesis® Basic Procedure about this detail again.

For example: I remove all my energy related to my biology teacher's beard and everything it represents!

Repeat the process for each window until the relative discomfort is low (1-2) or even 0 for all teachers. Then repeat the fourth sentence: *I attune, all my systems, to this new awareness.*

What I have observed from my experience with Professor Levy is that when you retrieve your energy from the other person and the events that are related to them, you feel more confident and free. These experiences with teachers can have a transforming effect on your confidence in studying and your self-esteem!

NOTES

Activity 2: When we perceived a feeling of intrusion

Sometimes we can feel our personal space is being invaded and we don't know how to react. We have found the other person to be too close, perceived as inappropriate, violent or ambiguous. Maybe we have been harassed or assaulted by someone larger than us.

For this exercise work on a person towards whom the discomfort is not too strong. For severe traumatic situations, it is essential to seek the help of a professional who can accompany you and give you a safe space to process the dramatic event.

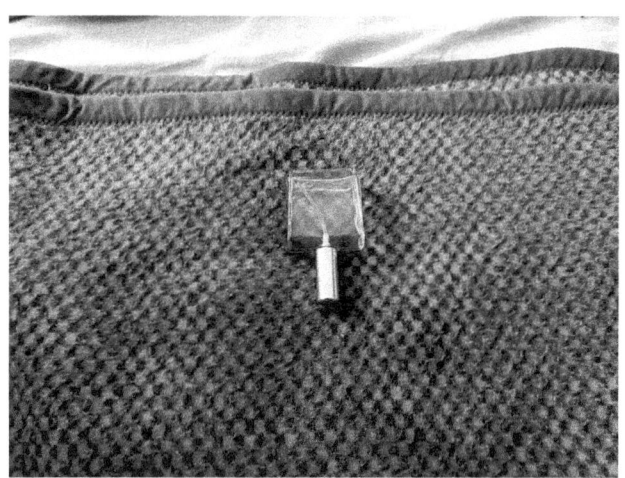

For this activity take a blanket, which will represent your personal space. Then get an object that symbolises the other person. I chose a small bottle of perfume to represent a person who had touched me inappropriately and used very strong scents.

Sit in the middle of the blanket. Place the object in your personal space. Observe what is happening in your body, your thoughts, your emotions. Rate the discomfort from 0 to 10.

Apply the sentences to this object and everything it represents.

Sentences of the Logosynthesis® Basic Procedure:

I retrieve, all my energy, bound up in X (the representation), and all it represents, and take it to the right place in myself. (Pause here to allow the words to work)

I remove, all non-me energy, related to X (the representation), and all it represents, from all my cells, all my body and my personal space, and send it where it truly belongs. (Pause here to allow the words to work)

I retrieve, all my energy, bound up in all my reactions, to X (the representation), and all it represents, and take it, to the right place in myself. (Pause here to allow the words to work)

Observe what has changed. Within your space, move the object if you feel it is necessary, and speak the sentences again about the object itself and all that it represents until you no longer feel it is intrusive, the object has become neutral, and it no longer causes you discomfort. Observe now how you feel in your personal space. What is your stress level? What is your confidence level?

Now think about the person and the episode you have been working on and observe what has changed.

When you get to 0, repeat the following sentence: *I attune, all my systems, to this new awareness.*

NOTES

YOURSELF & YOUR FUTURE

STUDIES

Activity 1: The mountain of things to do

What do you have to do for school? What homework have you been assigned? The books to read? The things to write and organise?

We often feel overwhelmed by the mountain of commitments and are emotionally disturbed by some tasks that worry us more than others, because they concern a subject that can be more complicated for us or because the exercise is difficult, long or tiring. Maybe we have a test ahead of us or we have to present work to the class or the teacher that is subject to the judgement of others or a school grade.

We can feel there is a lot at stake in studying!

Try to put on your table "a patchwork" of the works to be done that clutter your mind. I propose, to simplify the problem and lighten 'the task of homework', to put all the books and notebooks and materials you need on your desk. For example, if you have to do a work on Shakespeare, you can also add one of his books or a picture representing him or his theme. This is an exercise you can also do every day!

Once you have arranged everything on the table, observe what goes on inside you in front of this group of to-do's.

What are your emotions? What thoughts do you have? Where are the tensions in your body?

Rate from 0 to 10 how much discomfort you feel and apply the sentences of the Logosynthesis® Basic Procedure to the "to-do" group.

Sentences of the Logosynthesis® Basic Procedure:

I retrieve, all my energy, bound up in X (the representation), and all it represents, and take it to the right place in myself. (Pause here to allow the words to work)

I remove, all non-me energy, related to X (the representation), and all it represents, from all my cells, all my body and my personal space, and send it where it truly belongs. (Pause here to allow the words to work)

I retrieve, all my energy, bound up in all my reactions, to X (the representation), and all it represents, and take it, to the right place in myself. (Pause here to allow the words to work)

What has changed for you now? What is now your stress level from 0 to 10 in front of this "mountain" of tasks ?

If you are not at 0, observe the things on your desk and notice if your gaze focuses on a particular object that makes you uneasy, and say the sentences about this object. Once you get to 0 repeat the following: *I attune, all my systems, to this new awareness.*

Continue until you feel in harmony with the things you have to do and no longer perceive discomfort.

Now you can start! Happy studying!

NOTES

Activity 2: Fear of making mistakes

Making mistakes is fundamental in life. Mistakes are essential for us to learn. When we try something and we make a mistake, it is a useful way for us to realise that we have to take another path. We should actually celebrate every mistake we make because of what it teaches us. I love the phrase "win or learn", something either works out the way we hoped or we can learn from it and do something different in the future.

Unfortunately, at school the grade system prevents us from seeing errors as a positive thing and can lead us to fear them in exams and tests. We want to answer perfectly and can feel great pressure to try not to make mistakes.

Take a moment with this exercise to feel what happens in your body when you think about making a mistake. What are the emotions that come to you, also what are the thoughts? Give yourself time to explore what you fear, how it might occur and what memories or people are involved in your fear.

Then on a sheet of paper, create a representation of the authority figure (parent, teacher, etc) you feel compels you not to make a mistake. Put colours and shapes on it, and it doesn't matter if your drawing is beautiful or ugly, the important thing is to represent your discomfort, the pressure you feel when faced with a task to do because of the fear of making a mistake.

Rate the discomfort from 0 to 10 in relation to this drawing and the stress you feel.

How much do you believe from 0 to 10 that making a mistake is bad?

Start applying the sentences on the belief that to make a mistake is bad.

Rate from 0 to 10 how much you still believe it after saying the sentences.

Sentences of the Logosynthesis® Basic Procedure:

I retrieve, all my energy, bound up in X (the representation), and all it represents, and take it to the right place in myself. (Pause here to allow the words to work)

I remove, all non-me energy, related to X (the representation), and all it represents, from all my cells, all my body and my personal space, and send it where it truly belongs. (Pause here to allow the words to work)

I retrieve, all my energy, bound up in all my reactions, to X (the representation), and all it represents, and take it, to the right place in myself. (Pause here to allow the words to work)

Then, if you are not at 0, look at your drawing and note on it which part for you represents this idea that to make a mistake is "wrong". Is it the whole drawing? One part? A colour? A stroke? A detail of the character?

Rate from 0 to 10 how much stress it causes you and apply the sentences of the Logosynthesis® Basic Procedure to the design or detail that draws your attention.

If you are not at 0, check the drawing again: in what detail does your belief remain and how much stress does it cause you. Continue applying the sentences on each emotionally triggering detail until the drawing no longer causes you stress and the belief that getting it wrong is bad, is at 0. When you get to 0, repeat the following sentence: *I attune, all my systems, to this new awareness.*

What has changed now? How do you see the homework? The tests and exams? How can you deal with this material now? Observe what has changed.

NOTES

WORK

Activity 1: A "Good" Job

Sometimes we can be told or feel like the things we love can't make us any money so we should just focus on a "good career", a.k.a., a job that pays well. In my experience, if we don't do something we enjoy, the money, very quickly, doesn't make up for the dislike we have for the work. Many people I have worked with in their 40's and 50's are now looking to change their career as they want to do something they love.

Ideally, we will do what we love. As you work with Logosynthesis® you can become more and more in tune with what is meaningful and what matters to you. Take a moment to think about the things you enjoy and that make you feel good in life. Our passions are Our engine.

Now on a piece of paper, in the top centre, draw a circle and represent how you feel when you do these things that make you feel good.

At the bottom of the page, still in the centre, draw an X. This is you in the here and now. The circle represents the potential experience you can have in your work.

Now draw a line connecting the circle and X.

Then experience what happens when you have your hand resting on the "here and now X". What are the emotions, thoughts and beliefs you experience? What is your stress level from 0 to 10?

Touch the circle and experience the pulsating life inside you now. Feel yourself travelling through pleasant emotions, passions and thoughts about this potential future.

Take your finger back to the here and now and start to walk the line that connects it to the circle.
Start observing any tensions you feel along the way. Whenever you feel discomfort, stop on the line and notice any images, memories, sounds, smells, perceptions you have right now. Is it the voice of a parent or a teacher? Are you unsure if you can do it? Whatever the representation is, get a level of distress between 0-10 and then do the sentences of the Logosynthesis® Basic Procedure on it.

Sentences of the Logosynthesis® Basic Procedure:

I retrieve, all my energy, bound up in X (the representation), and all it represents, and take it to the right place in myself. (Pause here to allow the words to work)

I remove, all non-me energy, related to X (the representation), and all it represents, from all my cells, all my body and my personal space, and send it where it truly belongs. (Pause here to allow the words to work)

I retrieve, all my energy, bound up in all my reactions, to X (the representation), and all it represents, and take it, to the right place in myself. (Pause here to allow the words to work)

What has changed now? Observe what has changed and repeat the sentences with any new representations.

Once you get to 0, repeat the fourth sentence: *I attune, all my systems, to this new awareness.*

NOTES

Activity 2: The Family Business

It is important to understand that we are also influenced by what the adults around us do. I come from a family where you usually choose a job that you like and in which you can be comfortable and develop independently. The father of my children comes from a family that sees work as something boring and useless. Adults in the family environment can heavily influence our attitude to work with how they view and live in the world. The models we are in contact with can condition and influence us. Which models influence you?

Draw a symbol that represents you. Then, in the same way, draw the members of your family and write down their experiences and thoughts about work, as best as you can.
Look at the drawing and become aware of what it represents for you. What happens when you look at it? What emotions do you experience? What thoughts? Where is the discomfort located in your body, if any, and what is it connected to?

Then rate your stress level from 0 to 10 and apply the sentences of the Logosynthesis® Basic Procedure.

Sentences of the Logosynthesis® Basic Procedure:

I retrieve, all my energy, bound up in X (the representation), and all it represents, and take it to the right place in myself. (Pause here to allow the words to work)

I remove, all non-me energy, related to X (the representation), and all it represents, from all my cells, all my body and my personal space, and send it where it truly belongs. (Pause here to allow the words to work)

I retrieve, all my energy, bound up in all my reactions, to X (the representation), and all it represents, and take it, to the right place in myself. (Pause here to allow the words to work)

What has changed? What is your stress level from 0 to 10?

If you are not at 0, observe in your drawing who causes you the most stress and apply the sentences of the Logosynthesis® Basic Procedure to the person you have highlighted.

Observe the changes and the new stress level. If it is not at 0, repeat the procedure. When you get to 0, repeat the following sentence: *I attune, all my systems, to this new awareness.*

How do you see your potential job/career now? What might your dream job look like or be? What would you like for yourself?

NOTES

FUTURE ANXIETY

Activity 1: The disaster scenario

In our experience, a lot more young people are suffering from anxiety about the future: world events, our future prospects and so many other things that are outside of our control can weigh heavily on all of us. This anxiety can create fear within us.

The problem is that this fear can then block us. When I was young, I was afraid of being unemployed. That's why I went and studied areas that didn't actually fill my heart but were more likely to make it easy for me to find a job. In the end they were of no use to me in life except to give "truth" to my fear. But this same fear prevented me from connecting to what was really important to me, what I was good at, and what was right for me. Fear of the future can unnecessarily prevent you from taking action to achieve what you want. Since no one knows the future, you can't really know what's going to happen, it's only guesswork, and focusing solely on that is not productive!

Remember our Gremlin? Well, our Gremlin will tell us all the possible bad things that lie ahead of us if we try to change anything. We will hear it say things like, "You'll never get a job if you do that" or "That's way out of your league" but these are just beliefs that are not actual facts.

For this exercise, grab a large white sheet of paper, markers or coloured pencils, and draw a catastrophic scenario for your future. Represent everything that comes into your mind, let yourself go, write down the words that emerge in your thoughts, illustrate the different parts that give you discomfort.

Look at your drawing and what it represents. What happens when you see it? What emotions do you experience? What thoughts? Where is your discomfort located in your body and what is it related to?

Rate from 0 to 10 your level of stress related to the drawing and now apply the sentences of the Logosynthesis® Basic Procedure to the image and everything it represents.

Sentences of the Logosynthesis® Basic Procedure:

I retrieve, all my energy, bound up in X (the representation), and all it represents, and take it to the right place in myself. (Pause here to allow the words to work)

I remove, all non-me energy, related to X (the representation), and all it represents, from all my cells, all my body and my personal space, and send it where it truly belongs. (Pause here to allow the words to work)

I retrieve, all my energy, bound up in all my reactions, to X (the representation), and all it represents, and take it, to the right place in myself. (Pause here to allow the words to work)

What has changed? What is your stress level from 0 to 10?

If you are not at 0, observe what causes you the most stress, whether it is a feature, a colour, or a detail, and apply the sentences of the Logosynthesis® Basic Procedure on the detail you have highlighted.

Observe the changes and the new level of discomfort. If it is not at 0 repeat the process. Then repeat: *I attune, all my systems, to this new awareness.*

NOTES

Activity 2: The monster on the road

As we grow, we can all follow different paths and interests. Sometimes we want to go down a particular road (e.g. trying a new activity) but we stop ourselves and it can feel like there is something blocking the road ahead of us that will be too difficult to overcome. This can then prevent us from even trying. Let's work to remove the blockages on the path.

Let's make a visualisation of this scary future.

Sit comfortably and imagine a path leading into the future and that there is a monster blocking your way. Observe it. What kind of creature is it? What does it look like? What size is it? Describe it! What is your stress level from 0 to 10?

Then apply the sentences of the Logosynthesis® Basic Procedure on it.

Sentences of the Logosynthesis® Basic Procedure:

I retrieve, all my energy, bound up in X (the representation), and all it represents, and take it to the right place in myself. (Pause here to allow the words to work)

I remove, all non-me energy, related to X (the representation), and all it represents, from all my cells, all my body and my personal space, and send it where it truly belongs. (Pause here to allow the words to work)

I retrieve, all my energy, bound up in all my reactions, to X (the representation), and all it represents, and take it, to the right place in myself. (Pause here to allow the words to work)

What is your new level of discomfort from 0 to 10. Once you have deactivated your stress potential, what is the path like? What has changed? How do you view your future now? When you get to 0, repeat the following sentence: *I attune, all my systems, to this new awareness.*

You can make these monsters disappear whenever they appear, thanks to Logosynthesis®.

NOTES

LOVE

Activity 1: Getting closer to your love

When we like someone we can experience a mixture of excitement and fear. The emotions are strong and conflicting. On the one hand we would like to be close to the loved one, on the other hand we can have many doubts, insecurities and fears.

In this activity, let's observe what happens inside you when you get close to your "flame", whether it is a person you are already seeing or not, someone you have declared yourself to or not, and what happens when you get close to the person who makes your heart beat faster.

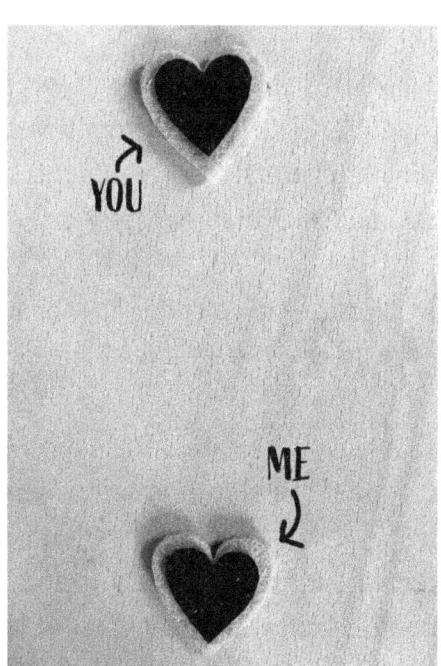

Start by making two little hearts. I made mine out of felt. You could make them out of cardboard, papers, Play-Doh (if you have a little brother or sister to steal it from!) or any other material. The size will be about 3 cm high.

Place the two little hearts in front of you following your feelings about their position in relation to each other: how far apart they should be and how they should be arranged.

Put one hand on the little heart that represents you and experience what you feel when you look at the other little heart. How much discomfort do you feel from 0 to 10? What are your emotions, what are your thoughts? Where do you experience them in your body?

And if this discomfort, these emotions and thoughts located in your body were an animal, what would it be? Stick with the one that comes to mind first.

For example in my position I feel fear, I think I can't make it and I feel a pain in my chest. If it were an animal, it would be an octopus!

How about you?

Now say the sentences for the animal you imagined and everything it represents, whether it's a rabbit that wants to escape or a snail that wants to retreat into its shell. For example, "I retrieve all my energy bound up in this octopus and all it represents..."

Sentences of the Logosynthesis® Basic Procedure:

I retrieve, all my energy, bound up in X (the representation), and all it represents, and take it to the right place in myself. (Pause here to allow the words to work)

I remove, all non-me energy, related to X (the representation), and all it represents, from all my cells, all my body and my personal space, and send it where it truly belongs. (Pause here to allow the words to work)

I retrieve, all my energy, bound up in all my reactions, to X (the representation), and all it represents, and take it, to the right place in myself. (Pause here to allow the words to work)

Now rate the level of discomfort again from 0 to 10, from your position looking at the other, and find out if you feel like moving your heart, closer or not, to the other. If there is still a worry or fear, think about a new animal that represents this emotion. Then say the sentences about the new animal that appears to you and all that it represents.

In my case, I didn't feel like moving it right away. First I spoke the sentences about a barking dog that had appeared to me after feeling sadness and having the thought that I suck and feeling a weight in my head.

Rate your discomfort again from 0 to 10, then figure out if you want to move your heart. When you get to 0, repeat the following sentence: *I attune, all my systems, to this new awareness.*

I moved it like in the picture and on my little heart I felt like the other one was a hedgehog whose quills I could feel. It was bothering me. I said the sentences about the hedgehog and everything it represented. You also go on following all the animals that appear to you connected to the various fears and discomforts you feel, until the moment you feel good next to each other.

NOTES

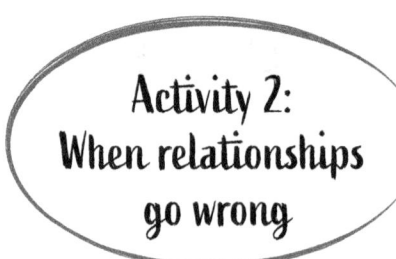

Activity 2: When relationships go wrong

Now let's try to explore what happened in a relationship or interaction, even when the interaction is only imaginary (during my adolescence I dreamt of many boys without daring to let them know).

How do you see yourself ? How do you see the other person? How do you see the relationship?

Grab some crayons. Make a coloured circle for you and one for the other person. Represent the interaction between the two of you with a graphic stroke of any shape and size you want. Let your feelings guide you.

Here for example is my representation. It's interesting to see the result. Looking at my drawing I feel completely invaded and assaulted and I see the other person frustrated and angry.

You can work with the sentences of the Logosynthesis® Basic Procedure to "neutralise" the relationship, if unpleasant, and prevent it from still having an impact in your life and future encounters.

Give your drawing a title. Now rate from 0 to 10 how much discomfort it creates for you. What are the emotions? What are the thoughts? Where are they located in the body ?

After writing the title on the drawing, apply the sentences to everything you see and what it represents.

Sentences of the Logosynthesis® Basic Procedure:

I retrieve, all my energy, bound up in X (the representation), and all it represents, and take it to the right place in myself. (Pause here to allow the words to work)

I remove, all non-me energy, related to X (the representation), and all it represents, from all my cells, all my body and my personal space, and send it where it truly belongs. (Pause here to allow the words to work)

I retrieve, all my energy, bound up in all my reactions, to X (the representation), and all it represents, and take it, to the right place in myself. (Pause here to allow the words to work)

What has changed ? What is your stress level now from 0 to 10 ?

If you are not at 0, observe in the drawing what is causing the stress now. For example I have a level 6 and what causes me discomfort are the blue lines on "me" orange ball. I will then apply the sentences on these blue lines above to my orange ball.

How about you?

Now apply the sentences to the detail that causes you the most discomfort.

Then re-evaluate your stress level, and if it is not yet at 0, continue to apply the sentences on the details that are still causing you discomfort. In my case the orange ball is brighter and stronger and I no longer see the blue lines. Now I am bothered by the small ball, the one that represents the other. I will then say the sentences about the representation of the blue and brown ball.

Continue the work until the stress is 0 and observe the changes in your perception of the drawing, yourself, each other and your relationship. Once you get to 0, repeat the fourth sentence: *I attune, all my systems, to this new awareness.*

You may see your energy change completely. After doing this exercise I felt more joyful and lighter and ready to move forward. The relationship as it was before is no longer a burden to me and I feel in the here and now, no longer tied to this dynamic and the energy of the other person. I am perfectly aligned, and more open to my actual current relationships.

You can of course repeat this exercise on other relationships and continue to " clear " your space.

NOTES

POTENTIAL

Activity 1: My vision board

It is important to have a vision of the future. It's not that we are saying you have to know what you will do in the future, but having an idea of how you might like your future to look can give you a good focus to begin to take the steps you need to get you on this path.

Get a blank sheet of paper. Start cutting out pictures from magazines or print some off from your computer that will help you to form a vision board of what you want for yourself.

Stick them on the paper. Now spend some time thinking about what might block you from actually realising this future. Once you have figured out what the blockage is, give it a rating from 0 to 10 in terms of the level of distress it causes you.

Say the sentences of the Logosynthesis® Basic Procedure on the representation and keep working until you get to a 0.

Sentences of the Logosynthesis® Basic Procedure:

I retrieve, all my energy, bound up in X (the representation), and all it represents, and take it to the right place in myself. (Pause here to allow the words to work)

I remove, all non-me energy, related to X (the representation), and all it represents, from all my cells, all my body and my personal space, and send it where it truly belongs. (Pause here to allow the words to work)

I retrieve, all my energy, bound up in all my reactions, to X (the representation), and all it represents, and take it, to the right place in myself. (Pause here to allow the words to work)

When you get to 0, repeat the following sentence: *I attune, all my systems, to this new awareness.*

NOTES

Activity 2: Walking towards your vision

Lay your collage from the previous exercise on the floor in the corner of your room. Stand on the opposite side and walk slowly towards the paper. Notice what is happening inside you. What are your emotions, thoughts, sensations?

Observe any tensions you feel on the path. Whenever you feel uneasy, stop and say the sentences of the Logosynthesis® Basic Procedure about the images, memories, sounds, smells, perceptions you have encountered on your way and that come to mind.

Sentences of the Logosynthesis® Basic Procedure:

I retrieve, all my energy, bound up in X (the representation), and all it represents, and take it to the right place in myself. (Pause here to allow the words to work)

I remove, all non-me energy, related to X (the representation), and all it represents, from all my cells, all my body and my personal space, and send it where it truly belongs. (Pause here to allow the words to work)

I retrieve, all my energy, bound up in all my reactions, to X (the representation), and all it represents, and take it, to the right place in myself. (Pause here to allow the words to work)

If nothing occurs, congratulations! Now you can explore how you can practically start to work towards the future you want.

NOTES

CONCLUSION

GUESS WHAT?!
THERE IS NO CONCLUSION,
YOU CAN DO THIS
FOREVER!!

What parents need to know.

We understand that most parents will say the one major hope they have for their children is that they are happy, healthy and have a sense of purpose. One of the best ways we can do this is to give our children the opportunity to learn that they have the ability to overcome setbacks and know that they are resilient. This workbook is one way of letting them figure things out for themselves, thus empowering them to manage their own mental health.

Over many years, Myriam and Allen have seen a wide range of different anxieties and worries among the young people they have worked with. Both are trained in a number of different theories and believe that Logosynthesis® is one of the easiest and most effective modalities around.

With many theories, the information can sometimes be a bit difficult to understand but when put into practice, can be quite simple. This is why the pair wanted to create an easy-to-use workbook for teens and children to help them begin to manage their own levels of anxiety or worry and remove the beliefs that block them from achieving their goals, be they small or significant.

This workbook will give your child the chance to learn one of the most powerful tools we have ever come across. It is easy to use and your child can return to this workbook as needed.

It is important for us to point out that this workbook is not a replacement for psychotherapy, counselling or coaching. If your child is really struggling, please do seek out professional help.

What is Logosynthesis®?

Created by Dr. Willem Lammers, a Dutch/Swiss psychologist, Logosynthesis® is a way to use words to heal trauma, remove negative beliefs and get rid of fears that many people experience. Most people have heard the phrase, "Sticks and stones will break my bones, but words will never hurt me", and actually, it just isn't true. Words have power and can influence us in ways that we may not even notice.

We are all born into this world as perfect little humans and then as we grow we learn how to survive in the world. As part of this growing up, we take on beliefs that can help us and also hinder us as we become adults. There will be positive beliefs such as, Don't Kill. Other beliefs can seem to be positive on the outside, Do Your Best, but a child might interpret this as, You must do THE best and if you don't, you're not good enough! These beliefs can stay with us throughout our lives and get in the way of us creating the future we would like.

Logosynthesis® uses the power of words to help remove these beliefs (or blockages as we also call them), which allow a person's energy to be in flow, and when our energy is in flow, we are better able to live a content, happy life. So whether you have troubling memories or thoughts, worries about exams or school, challenging relationships with friends or family, or physical symptoms of anxiety (stomach pain, unable to sleep etc), this workbook will give you a new way to manage stress and improve your life.

Get in Touch

Allen:
allen@cacoaching.ie

Myriam:
info@myriam-nordemann.com

More info on Logosynthesis:
https://www.logosynthesis.international/en/

ABOUT THE AUTHORS

Myriam:

Myriam Nordemann is a counselor, Master Practitioner and Logosynthesis® Instructor. She wrote the first Logosynthesis® book for children, *Willy and the Little Monsters*, published in English, French, Italian and German. Nordemann also holds a Master's degree in Couples Psychology and is a Parenting Consultant. She works online and runs workshops and seminars onsite and online.

Previously a journalist and interpreter for over 15 years in professional cycling, she is the author of *Ciclismo Mon Amour*, a humorous autobiographical story of her experience, experience which she now uses to help athletes improve their confidence and performance through Logosynthesis®.

Website:
www.myriam-nordemann.com

Allen:

Allen O'Donoghue is a qualified Logosynthesis® Practitioner who has been working with children and families for 25 years. With qualifications in Transactional Analysis Psychotherapy, Social Science and Business & Life Coaching, Allen's specialist knowledge and understanding of family dynamics has supported hundreds of young people and adults in setting and achieving their personal goals. This experience has brought Allen to become a highly regarded speaker on coaching, appearing regularly on radio and television and presenting at international events. Allen is also the author of the *Parenting in my Pocket* series of books.

Websites:
http://cacoaching.ie/
https://helpme2parent.ie

ACKNOWLEDGEMENTS

We want to thank every single client we have ever worked with. They have trusted us and allowed us to develop our skills and techniques.

We also want to thank Dr. Willem Lammers for creating such a powerfully gentle technique that is having such a profound impact on the world.

Thanks also go to our friends and families for the continued support and backing that we have received over the years.

And finally, thank YOU for picking up this workbook and committing to not being held back by anxiety!

DISCLAIMER:

The information contained in this book is educational in nature and is provided only as general information. Logosynthesis® is an innovative approach to healing and development, and the extent of its effectiveness, as well as its risks and benefits are not fully known. The reader agrees to assume and accept full responsibility for all risks associated with reading this book and using Logosynthesis® as a result. The reader understands that if he or she chooses to use Logosynthesis, emotional or physical sensations or additional unresolved memories may surface, which could be perceived as negative side effects. Emotional material may continue to surface after applying Logosynthesis® methods, indicating other issues may need to be addressed. Previously vivid or traumatic memories may fade which could adversely impact your ability to provide detailed legal testimony regarding a traumatic incident.

The information presented in this text is not intended to represent that Logosynthesis® is used to diagnose, treat, cure, or prevent any disease or psychological disorder. Logosynthesis® is not a substitute for medical or psychological treatment. The case reports and information presented in this text do not constitute a warranty, guarantee, or prediction regarding the outcome of an individual using Logosynthesis® for any issue. The authors make no warranty, guarantee, or prediction regarding any outcome for using Logosynthesis® for any issue. The information presented in this book is only for your own personal use,

To use Logosynthesis® with others, you need to become sufficiently trained and qualified as a Logosynthesis® Practitioner.

www.ingramcontent.com/pod-product-compliance
Lightning Source LLC
Chambersburg PA
CBHW081919090526
44591CB00015B/2401